Southern Living
★ ★ ★ ★ ★

Quick & Easy
Weeknight Favorites

Here are 10 of our favorite easy dinner menus. Each menu gives you an entrée and a side dish or dessert recipe; then we fill in with easy ideas for you to round out the meal. Along with each menu, look for a grocery list and prep plan that will provide an easy pace for getting dinner on the table.

weeknight menus

A Taste of Tex-Mex	2
Sunset Supper	4
Casual Night	6
Family-Pleasing Chicken	8
Italian Fare	10
Patio Supper	12
Splurge Supper	14
Before the Game	16
Faux-Fried Favorites	18
Soup and Sandwich Night	20

A Taste of Tex-Mex

Weeknight Enchiladas   refried beans

shredded lettuce with guacamole   **Toffee Surprise**

serves 4

Weeknight Enchiladas

prep: 7 minutes   cook: 29 minutes

1 pound ground chuck
1 small onion, chopped
1 (10¾-ounce) can tomato soup, undiluted
1 (10-ounce) can mild enchilada sauce
8 (7- or 8-inch) flour tortillas
2 cups (8 ounces) shredded Cheddar cheese, divided
Sour cream (optional)
Sliced ripe olives (optional)

Cook beef and onion in a large skillet over medium-high heat until meat is browned, stirring until it crumbles; drain and return to skillet.

Stir soup and enchilada sauce into meat mixture. Spread ¼ cup meat mixture onto each tortilla; sprinkle tortillas evenly with 1 cup cheese. Roll up tortillas; place, seam side down, in a greased 13- x 9-inch baking dish. Pour remaining meat mixture over tortillas.

Cover and bake at 350° for 20 minutes. Uncover and sprinkle with remaining 1 cup cheese; bake 5 more minutes or until cheese melts. If desired, serve with sour cream and olives. Yield: 4 servings.

Toffee Surprise

prep: 9 minutes

1 quart vanilla ice cream
4 (1¼-ounce) English toffee candy bars, coarsely crushed
¼ cup coffee liqueur

Spoon ice cream and crushed toffee bars evenly into 4 parfait glasses or dessert dishes. Just before serving, top each with 1 tablespoon liqueur. Yield: 4 servings.

menu plan

1. Prepare Toffee Surprise, but don't add liqueur; freeze until serving time.
2. Prepare and bake enchiladas.
3. While enchiladas bake, shred lettuce, and heat refried beans with green chiles in a saucepan over low heat.
4. Sprinkle cheese on enchiladas; bake 5 more minutes.
5. Top each dessert with liqueur just before serving.

groceries needed

- 1 pound ground chuck
- 1 small onion
- 1 (10¾-ounce) can tomato soup
- 1 (10-ounce) can mild enchilada sauce
- Package flour tortillas
- 8 ounces Cheddar cheese
- Sour cream
- Can sliced ripe olives
- 1 quart vanilla ice cream
- 4 (1¼-ounce) English toffee candy bars
- ¼ cup coffee liqueur
- 1 (16-ounce) can refried beans
- 1 (4.5-ounce) can chopped green chiles
- Lettuce
- Commercial guacamole

equipment needed

- Large skillet
- 13- x 9-inch baking dish
- Saucepan

Sunset Supper

Herbed Shrimp and Pasta   sliced tomatoes

Dilled Garlic Bread   pound cake

serves 6

Herbed Shrimp and Pasta

prep: 5 minutes   cook: 20 minutes

    8 ounces dried angel hair pasta, uncooked
    1 cup butter
1 ½ pounds peeled, medium-size fresh shrimp (2 pounds
       unpeeled)
    4 garlic cloves, minced
    2 cups half-and-half
  ½ cup chopped fresh parsley
  ½ teaspoon salt
  ¼ teaspoon pepper
    2 teaspoons chopped fresh dill or ¾ teaspoon dried
       dillweed (optional)
       Garnish: fresh dill sprigs

Cook pasta according to package directions. Drain;
set aside, and keep warm.
Meanwhile, melt butter in a large heavy skillet over
medium-high heat; add shrimp and garlic. Cook, stirring constantly, 3 to 5 minutes or until shrimp turn
pink. Remove shrimp, and set aside, reserving garlic
and butter in skillet.
Add half-and-half to skillet; bring to a boil, stirring
gently. Reduce heat, and simmer 15 minutes or until
thickened, stirring occasionally. Add shrimp, parsley,
salt, pepper, and, if desired, chopped dill; stir until
blended. Serve over pasta. Garnish, if desired. Yield:
6 servings.

Dilled Garlic Bread

prep: 10 minutes   cook: 10 minutes

  ⅓ cup butter or margarine, softened
  ¼ cup finely chopped fresh dill
    2 large cloves garlic, crushed
    1 (16-ounce) loaf unsliced French bread
  ¼ cup grated Parmesan cheese

Combine first 3 ingredients. Slice loaf in half length-
wise. Spread butter mixture evenly on cut sides of
bread. Sprinkle with cheese. Place on an ungreased
baking sheet. Bake at 375° for 10 minutes or until
browned. Slice and serve hot. Yield: 1 loaf.

menu plan

1. Bring pasta water to
a boil.
2. Soften butter for bread.
3. Cook pasta; keep warm.
4. While pasta cooks,
prepare shrimp cream
sauce.
5. Prepare and bake garlic
bread.
6. Slice tomatoes and
pound cake just before
serving.

groceries needed

Check staples: butter or
margarine, salt, pepper
* 8 ounces dried angel hair
pasta
* 1 ½ pounds peeled, medium-
size fresh shrimp
* Fresh garlic
* 2 cups half-and-half
* Bunch fresh parsley
* Bunch fresh dill
* 1 (16-ounce) loaf unsliced
French bread
* ¼ cup grated Parmesan
cheese
* Fresh tomatoes
* Pound cake

equipment needed

* Dutch oven
* Colander
* Large heavy skillet
* Baking sheet

Casual Night

Three-Pepper Pork Cutlets   rice pilaf with vegetables

fried apples   broccoli spears   **Cinnamon Ice Cream**

serves 4

Three-Pepper Pork Cutlets

prep: 10 minutes   cook: 8 minutes

1   (1-pound) pork tenderloin
1   teaspoon paprika
1   teaspoon dried thyme
½   teaspoon dried oregano
½   teaspoon dried rosemary, crushed
¼   teaspoon salt
¼   teaspoon ground white pepper
¼   teaspoon black pepper
⅛   teaspoon ground red pepper
1   teaspoon olive oil
2   garlic cloves, crushed

Cut pork crosswise into 12 slices. Place each pork slice between 2 sheets of heavy-duty plastic wrap, and flatten to ¼-inch thickness, using the heel of your hand or a meat mallet.

Combine paprika and next 9 ingredients; rub over both sides of pork slices. Place pork on a broiler rack coated with cooking spray; place rack in a broiler pan. Broil 5½ inches from heat 3 to 4 minutes on each side or until done. Yield: 4 servings.

Cinnamon Ice Cream

prep: 10 minutes

1   quart vanilla ice cream, slightly softened
1   teaspoon ground cinnamon
    Hot fudge topping

Stir together ice cream and cinnamon in a large bowl. Refreeze, if desired. Scoop into serving dishes, and drizzle with fudge topping. Yield: 4 servings.

menu plan

1. Soften ice cream, and stir in cinnamon; freeze until serving time.
2. Cook rice pilaf and broccoli according to package directions; keep warm.
3. While side dishes cook, prepare pork, and broil.
4. Heat apples in a saucepan over medium-low heat, if desired.
5. Scoop ice cream into serving dishes, and top with fudge sauce before serving dessert.

groceries needed

Check staples: paprika, dried thyme, dried oregano, dried rosemary, salt, ground white pepper, black pepper, ground red pepper, olive oil, vegetable cooking spray, ground cinnamon

- 1 pound pork tenderloin
- Fresh garlic
- 1 (16-ounce) bag frozen rice pilaf with vegetables
- 1 (28-ounce) jar fried apples
- 1 (16-ounce) package frozen broccoli spears
- 1 quart vanilla ice cream
- Hot fudge topping

equipment needed

- Meat mallet
- Broiler pan with rack
- Saucepan with lid

Family-Pleasing Chicken

Creamy Chicken Casserole

green beans   **Mandarin Orange and Lettuce Salad**   apple pie

serves 4

Creamy Chicken Casserole

prep: 5 minutes   cook: 30 minutes

3   cups chopped cooked chicken
1   (10¾-ounce) can cream of chicken soup, undiluted
1   (8-ounce) carton sour cream
1   tablespoon poppy seeds
1½ cups crushed round buttery crackers (40 crackers)
¼   cup butter or margarine, melted

Combine first 4 ingredients; spoon into a greased 11- x 7-inch baking dish. Combine crushed crackers and butter, and sprinkle over chicken mixture. Bake, uncovered, at 350° for 30 minutes. Yield: 4 servings.

Mandarin Orange and Lettuce Salad

prep: 5 minutes

6   cups torn mixed greens or 1 (16-ounce) package mixed lettuces
1   (11-ounce) can mandarin oranges, drained
⅓   cup golden raisins
1   (2-ounce) package cashew nuts, toasted (⅓ cup)
½   cup commercial Italian dressing or sweet-and-sour dressing

Combine first 4 ingredients in a salad bowl. Pour salad dressing over salad, and toss. Serve immediately. Yield: 4 servings.

menu plan

1. Prepare and bake chicken casserole.
2. While casserole bakes, trim and cook green beans, and toast cashews for salad.
3. Prepare salad.
4. Heat pie during dinner.

groceries needed

Check staples: poppy seeds, butter or margarine

* 3 cups chopped cooked chicken
* 1 (10¾-ounce) can cream of chicken soup
* 1 (8-ounce) carton sour cream
* Round buttery crackers
* 6 cups torn mixed greens or 1 (16-ounce) package mixed lettuces
* 1 (11-ounce) can mandarin oranges
* ⅓ cup golden raisins
* 1 (2-ounce) package cashew nuts (⅓ cup)
* Commercial Italian or sweet-and-sour dressing
* 1½ pounds fresh or frozen green beans
* Commercial apple pie

equipment needed

* 11- x 7-inch baking dish
* Saucepan

Italian Fare

Quick Carbonara

green salad   rolls   **Simple Tiramisù**

serves 4

Quick Carbonara

prep: 10 minutes   cook: 19 minutes

1 (8-ounce) package dried spaghetti, uncooked
8 slices bacon
⅔ cup chopped green onions
1 (4-ounce) can sliced mushrooms, drained
3 egg yolks, lightly beaten
1½ cups (6 ounces) finely shredded Cheddar cheese
    Dash of pepper

Cook pasta according to package directions. Meanwhile, cook bacon in a large skillet until crisp; remove bacon, reserving 3 tablespoons drippings in skillet. Coarsely crumble bacon, and set aside.

Cook green onions and mushrooms in drippings in skillet over medium heat 2 minutes. Drain pasta, and place in a serving bowl. Stir egg yolks into hot pasta immediately after draining it. Stir in bacon, green onions and mushrooms, cheese, and pepper; toss. Serve immediately. Yield: 4 servings.

Simple Tiramisù

prep: 15 minutes   freeze: 30 minutes

1 (8-ounce) package cream cheese, softened
¾ cup strong brewed coffee, cooled
3 (1-ounce) squares semisweet chocolate, grated
¾ cup chopped almonds, toasted and divided
1 (12-ounce) container frozen whipped topping, thawed
2 (3-ounce) packages ladyfingers, split

Beat cream cheese in a large bowl at high speed of an electric mixer until fluffy. Add ¼ cup coffee, beating until blended. Stir in grated chocolate and ½ cup almonds. Set aside 1 cup whipped topping. Fold remaining whipped topping into cream cheese mixture.

Brush cut sides of ladyfingers with remaining ½ cup coffee. Arrange two-thirds of ladyfingers on bottom and up sides of a 2-quart bowl (such as a large mixing bowl); spoon cream cheese mixture into center. Top with remaining ladyfingers and reserved 1 cup whipped topping; sprinkle with remaining ¼ cup almonds. Cover and freeze 30 minutes. Yield: 8 servings.

menu plan

1. Bring pasta water to a boil.
2. Prepare tiramisù; freeze until serving time.
3. Cook pasta. Cook bacon.
4. While pasta cooks, toss salad ingredients, and finish preparing carbonara.
5. Heat rolls in oven according to package directions, if desired.

groceries needed

Check staples: 3 egg yolks, pepper
- 1 (8-ounce) package dried spaghetti
- 8 slices bacon
- Bunch green onions
- 1 (4-ounce) can sliced mushrooms
- 6 ounces Cheddar cheese
- 1 (8-ounce) package cream cheese
- Coffee
- 3 to 4 (1-ounce) squares semisweet chocolate
- ¾ cup chopped almonds
- 1 (12-ounce) container frozen whipped topping
- 2 (3-ounce) packages ladyfingers
- Makings for green salad
- Crusty rolls

equipment needed
- Dutch oven
- Colander
- Large skillet
- Electric mixer
- Pastry brush

Patio Supper

Sausage-Stuffed French Loaf   Cucumber-Tomato Salad

potato chips   chocolate chip cookies

serves 4

Sausage-Stuffed French Loaf

prep: 11 minutes   cook: 29 minutes

1 (16-ounce) loaf unsliced French bread
½ pound ground pork sausage
½ pound ground chuck
1 medium onion, chopped
2 cups (8 ounces) shredded mozzarella cheese
1 large egg, lightly beaten
¼ cup chopped fresh parsley
2 tablespoons Dijon mustard
½ teaspoon fennel seeds
½ teaspoon salt
¼ teaspoon pepper
2 tablespoons butter or margarine
1 large garlic clove, crushed

Cut off ends of loaf; set ends aside. Hollow out loaf with a long serrated bread knife, leaving a ½-inch shell. Process bread removed from inside loaf in a food processor to make coarse crumbs.

Cook sausage, beef, and onion in a large skillet until meat is browned, stirring until it crumbles; drain. Stir in 1 cup breadcrumbs, cheese, and next 6 ingredients. Spoon into shell; replace loaf ends, securing with wooden picks.

Melt butter in a saucepan. Add garlic; cook 1 minute. Brush garlic butter over loaf. Wrap loaf in foil, leaving top open slightly; place on a baking sheet. Bake at 400° for 25 minutes. Cut into 4 pieces. Yield: 4 servings.

Cucumber-Tomato Salad

prep: 8 minutes

3 tablespoons olive oil   ⅓ cup sliced ripe olives
1½ tablespoons lemon juice   2 tomatoes, cut into wedges
1 teaspoon Dijon mustard   1 cucumber, sliced
⅛ teaspoon salt   Lettuce leaves

Combine first 4 ingredients, stirring well with a fork or small whisk. Combine olives, tomato, and cucumber in a bowl. Pour dressing mixture over tomato mixture; toss. Cover and chill 30 minutes, if desired. Serve on lettuce leaves. Yield: 4 servings.

menu plan

1. Bake cookies according to package directions up to 1 day ahead.
2. Prepare and bake stuffed sausage loaf.
3. While loaf bakes, prepare salad; cover and chill.

groceries needed

Check staples: egg, Dijon mustard, fennel seeds, salt, pepper, butter or margarine, olive oil

- 1 (16-ounce) loaf unsliced French bread
- ½ pound ground pork sausage
- ½ pound ground chuck
- 1 medium onion
- 8 ounces mozzarella cheese
- Bunch fresh parsley
- Fresh garlic
- 1½ tablespoons lemon juice
- ⅓ cup sliced ripe olives
- 2 tomatoes
- 1 medium cucumber
- Lettuce leaves
- Potato chips
- Refrigerated chocolate chip cookie dough

equipment needed

- Serrated bread knife
- Food processor (optional)
- Large skillet
- Small saucepan
- Pastry brush
- Baking sheet

Splurge Supper

Filet Mignon with Horseradish Gravy

mashed potatoes   steamed asparagus   **Greek Salad**

French bread   commercial cheesecake

serves 4

Filet Mignon with Horseradish Gravy

prep: 2 minutes   cook: 20 minutes

4 (5-ounce) beef tenderloin steaks
¼ teaspoon salt
¼ teaspoon pepper
1 (¾-ounce) package brown gravy mix
½ cup water
½ cup red wine
2½ tablespoons prepared horseradish
1 (8-ounce) package sliced fresh mushrooms

Heat a heavy nonstick skillet over medium-high heat until hot. Sprinkle steaks with salt and pepper. Add steaks to hot skillet; cook 1 minute on each side. Place steaks in a greased small baking dish.

Add gravy mix and next 3 ingredients to skillet. Bring to a boil; reduce heat, and simmer, stirring constantly, until thickened. Stir in mushrooms. Pour mixture over steaks. Bake, uncovered, at 350° for 15 minutes or to desired doneness. Yield: 4 servings.

Greek Salad

prep: 14 minutes

1 medium head iceberg lettuce, torn
1 small purple onion, thinly sliced
½ cup pepperoncini salad peppers
½ cup kalamata olives
4 ounces crumbled feta cheese
½ cup commercial red wine vinaigrette

Combine all ingredients in a salad bowl; toss gently. Serve immediately. Yield: 4 servings.

menu plan

1. Thaw cheesecake according to package directions.
2. Prepare filet mignon recipe.
3. Microwave potatoes; then mash them. (Or prepare instant mashed potatoes according to package directions.)
4. While steaks cook, trim and steam asparagus in a small amount of boiling water 6 to 8 minutes.
5. Toss salad at the last minute.

groceries needed

Check staples: salt, pepper, prepared horseradish
- 4 (5-ounce) beef tenderloin steaks
- 1 (¾-ounce) package brown gravy mix
- Red wine
- 1 (8-ounce) package sliced fresh mushrooms
- 1 head iceberg lettuce
- 1 small purple onion
- ½ cup pepperoncini salad peppers
- ½ cup kalamata olives
- 4 ounces feta cheese
- Red wine vinaigrette
- 4 baking potatoes or 1 box of instant mashed potatoes
- 1 pound fresh asparagus
- French bread
- Frozen cheesecake

equipment needed
- Heavy nonstick skillet
- Small baking dish
- Asparagus steamer

Before the Game

Speedy Chili Dogs **Easy Coleslaw**

potato chips   brownies

serves 8

Speedy Chili Dogs

prep: 5 minutes   cook: 35 minutes

1   pound ground chuck
1   large onion, chopped (2 cups)
1   garlic clove, crushed
1   (15-ounce) can tomato sauce
2   tablespoons chili powder
¼   teaspoon salt
⅛   teaspoon pepper
1   cup water
8   frankfurters, cooked
8   hot dog buns, split and toasted
2   cups (8 ounces) shredded mild Cheddar cheese
Chopped green onions

Combine first 3 ingredients in a large skillet, and cook over medium-high heat until beef is browned, stirring until it crumbles; drain. Add tomato sauce and next 4 ingredients. Bring to a boil; cover, reduce heat, and simmer 25 minutes, stirring occasionally.

Place frankfurters in buns. Spoon chili mixture over frankfurters; top with cheese and green onions. Yield: 8 servings.

Easy Coleslaw

prep: 2 minutes

1   (16-ounce) package coleslaw
1   (8-ounce) bottle coleslaw dressing*
¼   teaspoon salt
¼   teaspoon pepper

Combine all ingredients in a large bowl, tossing well. Serve immediately, or cover and chill. Yield: 6 cups.

*For coleslaw dressing, we used Kraft.

menu plan

1. Prepare coleslaw.
   Chill, if desired.
2. Cook ground beef
   mixture for chili dogs.
3. While beef mixture
   simmers, cook frankfurters.
4. Split and toast buns;
   assemble chili dogs.

groceries needed

Check staples: chili powder, salt, pepper
- 1 pound ground chuck
- 1 large onion
- Fresh garlic
- 1 (15-ounce) can tomato sauce
- 8 frankfurters
- 8 hot dog buns
- 8 ounces mild Cheddar cheese
- Bunch green onions
- Potato chips
- 1 (16-ounce) package coleslaw
- 1 (8-ounce) bottle coleslaw dressing
- Brownies from a deli bakery

equipment needed
- Large skillet with lid
- Large saucepan

Faux-Fried Favorites

Oven-Fried Fish

zesty French fries   turnip greens   corn on the cob

Lemon Frappé

serves 4

Oven-Fried Fish

prep: 5 minutes   cook: 10 minutes

¼ cup white cornmeal
¼ cup fine, dry breadcrumbs
½ teaspoon salt
½ teaspoon paprika
1½ teaspoons chopped fresh dill or ½ teaspoon
    dried dillweed
⅛ teaspoon pepper
1 pound fresh or frozen fish fillets, thawed
⅓ cup milk
3 tablespoons butter or margarine, melted
Lemon wedges
Tartar sauce

Combine first 6 ingredients in a shallow dish. Dip fish fillets in milk, and dredge in cornmeal mixture. Place coated fish in a lightly greased 13- x 9-inch pan; drizzle with butter.
Bake at 450° for 10 minutes or until fish flakes easily when tested with a fork. Serve with lemon wedges and tartar sauce. Yield: 4 servings.

Lemon Frappé

prep: 4 minutes

1 (6-ounce) can frozen lemonade concentrate,
    undiluted
½ cup cold water
1 pint lemon sherbet or vanilla ice cream*
1 (12-ounce) can ginger ale

Combine first 3 ingredients in container of an electric blender; process until smooth, stopping once to scrape down sides. Pour into a serving pitcher; add ginger ale. Serve immediately. Yield: 4 cups.

*Plenty of lemon flavor prevails if you use vanilla ice cream in this slushy dessert beverage. To make a Lime Frappé, use a 6-ounce can limeade in place of lemonade concentrate.

menu plan

1. Bake French fries according to package directions. Bring water to a boil for corn, if cooking fresh ears.
2. Microwave turnip greens according to package directions; boil fresh corn, or cook frozen corn according to package directions.
3. While fries bake, prepare fish. Add fish to bake in oven during last 10 minutes fries bake.
4. Blend frappé after dinner.

groceries needed

Check staples: cornmeal, salt, paprika, pepper, milk, butter or margarine
- Fine, dry breadcrumbs
- Fresh or dried dillweed
- 1 pound fresh or frozen fish fillets
- 1 or 2 lemons
- Tartar sauce
- 1 (32-ounce) bag frozen French fries (we used Ore-Ida Zesties)
- 1 (10- or 16-ounce) package frozen turnip greens
- 4 ears of corn or 1 (16-ounce) package frozen corn
- 1 (6-ounce) can frozen lemonade concentrate
- 1 pint lemon sherbet or vanilla ice cream
- 1 (12-ounce) can ginger ale

equipment needed

- Shallow dish
- 13- x 9-inch pan
- Electric blender
- Baking sheet

Soup and Sandwich Night

Cream of Pimiento Soup

Grilled Ham and Cheese

serves 4

Cream of Pimiento Soup

prep: 2 minutes   cook: 20 minutes

1 (4-ounce) jar diced pimiento, undrained
3 tablespoons butter or margarine
3 tablespoons all-purpose flour
1 (14½-ounce) can ready-to-serve chicken broth
1½ cups half-and-half
2 teaspoons grated onion
½ teaspoon salt
¼ teaspoon hot sauce
Garnish: sour cream

Place pimiento in a blender; process until smooth, stopping once to scrape down sides. Set aside.

Melt butter in a heavy saucepan over low heat; add flour, stirring until smooth. Cook, stirring constantly, 1 minute. Gradually add broth and half-and-half to saucepan; cook over medium heat, stirring constantly, until thickened and bubbly.

Stir in pimiento, onion, salt, and hot sauce; cook over medium-low heat, stirring constantly, until heated. Garnish, if desired. Yield: 3½ cups.

Grilled Ham and Cheese

prep: 8 minutes   cook: 4 minutes

1 cup (4 ounces) shredded Monterey Jack cheese
1 cup (4 ounces) shredded Cheddar cheese
¼ cup mayonnaise
1 tablespoon prepared mustard
1 green onion, finely chopped
8 slices sandwich bread
4 slices sandwich ham
¼ cup butter or margarine, softened

Combine first 5 ingredients. Spread cheese mixture over 4 bread slices. Top each with a ham slice; top with remaining bread slices. Spread half of butter on tops of sandwiches. Invert sandwiches onto a hot nonstick skillet or griddle; cook over medium heat until browned. Spread remaining butter on ungrilled sides of sandwiches; turn and cook until browned. Yield: 4 servings.

menu plan

1. Prepare soup; keep warm.
2. Assemble sandwiches; grill sandwiches just before serving.

groceries needed

Check staples: butter or margarine, all-purpose flour, salt, hot sauce, mayonnaise, prepared mustard

- 1 (4-ounce) jar diced pimiento
- 1 (14½-ounce) can ready-to-serve chicken broth
- 1½ cups half-and-half
- Small onion
- Sour cream
- 4 ounces Monterey Jack cheese
- 4 ounces Cheddar cheese
- 1 green onion
- 8 slices bread
- Sandwich ham

equipment needed

- Electric blender
- Heavy saucepan
- Nonstick skillet or griddle

our favorite entrées

Here are two dozen more of our most popular main dishes ideal for busy weeknights. Enjoy a variety of entrées ranging from beef to shrimp to vegetarian. Look for food facts following each recipe.

Steak in Pepper Cream	23
Shortcut Lasagna	24
Oriental Burgers	25
Sweet Sloppy Joes	26
Texas Stew	27
Mushroom-Veal Marsala	28
Hunan Pork and Zucchini Stir-Fry	29
Molasses-Grilled Pork Tenderloin	30
Sweet Jalapeño Ribs	31
Grilled Ham and Apples	32
Creamy Ham Casserole	33
Toasted Almond Chicken	34
Chicken Parmigiana	35
Chicken-Almond Stir-Fry	36
Paella	37
Chicken Caesar Salad	38
Nacho Chicken	39
Turkey Pie	40
Salmon Bake with Pecan-Crunch Coating	41
Catfish Meunière	42
Shrimp Creole	43
Artichoke and Shrimp Linguine	44
Scallops in Vermouth Cream	45
Black Beans and Yellow Rice	46
Tortilla Pie	47
Index	48

Steak in Pepper Cream

prep: 3 minutes   cook: 19 minutes

¼ teaspoon salt
2 (12-ounce) New York strip steaks (¾ inch thick)
1½ tablespoons green peppercorns in liquid, drained
2 tablespoons steak sauce
2 tablespoons water
1 cup whipping cream
¼ teaspoon ground pepper

Place a 10-inch cast-iron skillet over medium heat until hot; sprinkle salt in skillet. Place steaks over salt; cook 4 minutes on each side or until browned. Remove from skillet.

Combine peppercorns, steak sauce, and water in hot skillet; cook over medium heat, stirring constantly, to loosen browned bits from bottom of skillet. Stir in whipping cream and pepper.

Bring to a boil; reduce heat, and simmer, stirring constantly, 3 to 4 minutes or until slightly thickened. Add steaks; simmer 5 minutes or to desired doneness, stirring occasionally. Yield: 2 to 4 servings.

***

Green peppercorns can be found in small jars on the grocery shelf along with the pickles.

Shortcut Lasagna

prep: 15 minutes   cook: 45 minutes

 1 pound ground beef
 2 large garlic cloves, crushed
 1 (28-ounce) jar spaghetti sauce
 ½ cup water
 1 large egg, lightly beaten
 1 (12-ounce) container cottage cheese
1½ teaspoons pepper
 8 lasagna noodles, uncooked
 1 (10-ounce) package frozen chopped spinach, thawed
    and drained
 2 cups (8 ounces) shredded mozzarella cheese
 ½ cup grated Parmesan cheese

Crumble beef into a 2-quart glass bowl; add garlic. Microwave at HIGH 6 minutes or until browned, stirring beef once; drain. Stir in spaghetti sauce and water. Combine egg, cottage cheese, and pepper.

Spread ½ cup meat sauce in a 13- x 9-inch baking dish. Top with half each of uncooked noodles, cottage cheese mixture, spinach, meat sauce, and mozzarella cheese. Repeat layers, and cover with heavy-duty plastic wrap.

Microwave at HIGH 8 minutes; then microwave at MEDIUM (50% power) 30 to 32 minutes or until noodles are tender, turning dish occasionally.

Sprinkle with Parmesan cheese; cover and let stand 15 minutes before serving. Yield: 6 servings.

The shortcut? Not cooking the noodles before layering them. They soften as they bake in the lasagna.

Oriental Burgers

prep: 11 minutes   grill: 12 minutes

1 pound ground chuck
⅓ cup chopped water chestnuts
¼ cup chopped green pepper
1 tablespoon brown sugar
2 tablespoons water
1 tablespoon lemon juice
1 tablespoon soy sauce
½ teaspoon ground ginger
2 green onions, finely chopped
4 sesame seed hamburger buns
Lettuce leaves
1 small white or purple onion, sliced
Hoisin Ketchup

Combine first 9 ingredients; shape into 4 patties.
Coat grill rack with cooking spray; place rack on grill over medium-high heat (350° to 400°). Place patties on rack; grill, uncovered, 5 to 6 minutes on each side or until done.
Place patties on buns with lettuce and onion. Spoon Hoisin Ketchup evenly over burgers. Yield: 4 servings.

Hoisin Ketchup

¼ cup ketchup
¼ cup hoisin sauce

Combine ketchup and hoisin sauce. Yield: ½ cup.

Hoisin sauce is a **thick, sweet and spicy sauce** used in Chinese cooking. Find it in Asian markets and many large supermarkets.

Sweet Sloppy Joes

prep: 5 minutes   cook: 23 minutes

1½ pounds ground beef
1 small onion, chopped
1 small green pepper, seeded and chopped
1 (10¾-ounce) can tomato soup, undiluted
1 (8-ounce) can tomato sauce
1 cup ketchup
2 tablespoons brown sugar
1 tablespoon Worcestershire sauce
1 teaspoon prepared mustard
⅛ teaspoon garlic powder
4 sesame seed hamburger buns, toasted

Cook first 3 ingredients in a large skillet until beef is browned, stirring until it crumbles; drain. Stir in soup and next 6 ingredients; simmer 10 to 15 minutes, stirring often. Serve on toasted buns. Yield: 4 servings.

For a menu partner, pop commercial frozen onion rings into the oven while the sloppy joe mixture simmers.

Texas Stew

prep: 5 minutes   slow cook: about 5½ to 10½ hours

2 pounds beef tips, cut into 1-inch pieces
1 (14½-ounce) can Mexican-style stewed tomatoes, undrained
1 (10½-ounce) can condensed beef broth, undiluted
1 (8-ounce) jar medium or mild picante sauce
1 (10-ounce) package frozen whole kernel corn
3 carrots, cut into ½-inch slices
1 medium onion, cut into thin wedges
2 cloves garlic, minced
1 teaspoon ground cumin
½ teaspoon salt
⅓ cup water
¼ cup all-purpose flour

Combine first 10 ingredients in a 3- or 4-quart electric slow cooker. Cover and cook on HIGH 5 hours or on LOW 10 hours or until meat is tender.

Combine water and flour, stirring until smooth; stir into meat mixture in slow cooker. Cook stew, uncovered, on HIGH 15 minutes or until thickened, stirring often. Yield: 10 cups.

Let your slow cooker **cook dinner while you work.** Just heat some bread to serve alongside when you get home.

Mushroom-Veal Marsala

prep: 6 minutes   cook: 13 minutes

1 teaspoon chopped fresh or dried rosemary
½ teaspoon salt
½ teaspoon freshly ground pepper
1 pound (¼-inch-thick) veal scaloppine
2 tablespoons olive oil
1 (8-ounce) package sliced fresh mushrooms
2 garlic cloves, minced
2 teaspoons cornstarch
1 teaspoon chicken bouillon granules
⅔ cup water
⅓ cup dry Marsala wine

Rub first 3 ingredients over veal. Heat oil in a large nonstick skillet over medium heat. Add half of veal; cook 2 minutes on each side or until lightly browned. Remove veal from skillet; keep warm. Repeat with remaining veal.

Add sliced mushrooms and garlic to skillet; cook over medium-high heat, stirring constantly, 3 minutes or until tender.

Combine cornstarch and remaining 3 ingredients; add to skillet. Cook, stirring constantly, 1 minute or until thick and bubbly. Serve over veal. Yield: 4 servings.

Marsala is a **smoky-flavored** Italian wine.

Hunan Pork and Zucchini Stir-Fry

prep: 11 minutes   cook: 10 minutes

¼ cup cornstarch
¼ cup water
1 pound boneless pork, cut into thin strips
3 tablespoons vegetable oil, divided
3 small zucchini, sliced (about 3 cups)
⅓ cup Hunan sauce
1 tablespoon sesame seeds, toasted
Hot cooked rice

Combine cornstarch and water, stirring until smooth. Add pork, tossing well. Heat 2 tablespoons oil in a large skillet over medium-high heat until hot. Add pork mixture; stir-fry 3 minutes or until pork is no longer pink. Remove from skillet. Heat remaining 1 tablespoon oil in skillet. Add zucchini; stir-fry 3 minutes or until tender.

Return pork to skillet; add Hunan sauce and sesame seeds. Stir-fry until thoroughly heated. Serve over rice. Yield: 4 servings.

If you can't find Hunan Sauce at a cook store or specialty grocery store, **substitute hoisin sauce or a stir-fry sauce.**

Molasses-Grilled Pork Tenderloin

prep: 5 minutes   marinate: 8 hours   grill: 20 minutes

- ½ cup molasses
- ¼ cup coarse-grained Dijon mustard
- 2 tablespoons apple cider vinegar or white vinegar
- 1 teaspoon salt
- 4 (¾-pound) pork tenderloins

Combine first 4 ingredients; brush half of mixture over pork. Cover and chill 8 hours. Chill remaining molasses glaze.

Coat grill rack with cooking spray; place on grill over medium-high heat (350° to 400°). Place pork on rack; grill, covered with grill lid, 18 to 20 minutes or until a meat thermometer inserted into thickest portion registers 160°, turning once and basting with reserved molasses glaze during last 8 minutes. Yield: 8 servings.

Looking for a shortcut? Grill the tenderloins as soon as you've glazed them. **You don't have to marinate them.**

Sweet Jalapeño Ribs

prep: 30 minutes   slow cook: 5½ to 10½ hours

2 (16-ounce) cans pinto beans, drained
3 pounds country-style pork ribs, trimmed
½ teaspoon garlic powder
½ teaspoon salt
½ teaspoon pepper
1 medium onion, chopped
1 (10.5-ounce) jar red jalapeño jelly
1 (5-ounce) bottle steak sauce*
2 jalapeño peppers, seeded and finely chopped
   (optional)

Place beans in a 4-quart electric slow cooker. Set aside.

Cut ribs apart; sprinkle with garlic powder, salt, and ½ teaspoon pepper. Place ribs on a rack in a broiler pan. Broil 5½ inches from heat 18 to 20 minutes or until well browned, turning once. Add ribs to slow cooker, and sprinkle with onion.

Combine jelly, steak sauce, and, if desired, chopped pepper in a saucepan; cook over low heat until jelly melts. Pour over ribs; stir gently.

Cover and cook on HIGH 5 to 6 hours or on LOW 9 to 10 hours. Remove ribs; skim fat from sauce. Cook sauce with beans, uncovered, on HIGH 30 more minutes or until slightly thickened. Add ribs just before serving to reheat. Yield: 4 servings.

*For steak sauce, we used A-1.

Broiling the ribs first browns them, adds **rich flavor,** and removes excess fat.

Grilled Ham and Apples

prep: 7 minutes   grill: 10 minutes

½ cup orange marmalade
2 teaspoons butter or margarine
¼ teaspoon ground ginger
2 (½-inch-thick) ham slices (about 2½ pounds)
4 small Granny Smith apples, cored and cut into
      4 rings each

Combine first 3 ingredients in a 1-cup glass measuring cup; microwave at HIGH 1 minute or until melted, stirring once.

Coat grill rack with cooking spray; place on grill over medium-high heat (350° to 400°). Place ham and apple rings on rack; grill, uncovered, 10 minutes or until apple rings are tender, turning and basting often with marmalade mixture. Yield: 6 to 8 servings.

Leave the peel on the apples for **pretty color.**

Creamy Ham Casserole

prep: 10 minutes   cook: 35 minutes

4 ounces dried medium egg noodles, uncooked
2 cups chopped cooked ham
1 medium-size green bell pepper, seeded and chopped
¼ cup chopped onion
¼ cup sliced celery
1 tablespoon vegetable oil
1 (10¾-ounce) can cream of mushroom soup, undiluted
1 (8-ounce) carton sour cream
½ cup (2 ounces) shredded Cheddar cheese

Cook pasta according to package directions; drain.
Cook ham and next 3 ingredients in oil in a large skil-
let over medium-high heat 5 minutes, stirring often.
Remove from heat; stir in soup, sour cream, and pasta.
Spoon into a lightly greased 1½-quart baking dish.
Cover and bake at 350° for 25 minutes. Sprinkle with
cheese, and bake, uncovered, 5 more minutes. Let
stand 10 minutes before serving. Yield: 4 servings.

Here's a great way to **use leftover ham.**

Toasted Almond Chicken

prep: 10 minutes   cook: 16 minutes

6   skinned and boned chicken breast halves
⅛   teaspoon salt
⅛   teaspoon black pepper
3   tablespoons butter or margarine, divided
1½ cups whipping cream
2   tablespoons orange marmalade
1   tablespoon Dijon mustard
⅛   teaspoon ground red pepper
1   (2.25-ounce) package sliced almonds, toasted

Place chicken between 2 sheets of heavy-duty plastic wrap, and flatten to ¼-inch thickness, using a meat mallet or rolling pin. Sprinkle with salt and black pepper.

Melt 1½ tablespoons butter in a large skillet over medium-high heat. Add half of chicken, and cook 2 minutes on each side or until golden. Remove chicken from skillet. Repeat procedure with remaining butter and chicken.

Reduce heat to medium; add whipping cream and next 3 ingredients to skillet, stirring well. Add chicken; sprinkle with almonds, and cook 8 minutes or until sauce thickens. Yield: 6 servings.

See this **golden entrée** photographed on the front cover.

Chicken Parmigiana

prep: 12 minutes   cook: 24 minutes

4   skinned and boned chicken breast halves
½   cup Italian-seasoned breadcrumbs
½   cup grated Parmesan cheese
1   large egg, lightly beaten
2   tablespoons butter or margarine
1   (14-ounce) jar spaghetti sauce (about 2 cups)
1   cup (4 ounces) shredded mozzarella cheese

Place chicken between 2 sheets of heavy-duty plastic wrap, and flatten to ¼-inch thickness, using a meat mallet or rolling pin.
Combine breadcrumbs and Parmesan cheese. Dip chicken in beaten egg; dredge in breadcrumb mixture.
Melt butter in a large skillet over medium-high heat; add chicken, and brown on each side. Arrange chicken in a lightly greased 11- x 7-inch baking dish. Pour spaghetti sauce over chicken, and sprinkle with mozzarella cheese. Cover and bake at 375° for 20 minutes or until thoroughly heated. Yield: 4 servings.

Use your favorite brand of spaghetti sauce in this recipe—**the spicier the better.**

Chicken-Almond Stir-Fry

prep: 6 minutes   cook: 10 minutes

2 tablespoons vegetable or sesame oil
4 skinned and boned chicken breast halves, cut into thin
    strips
1 (2.25-ounce) package sliced almonds
1 (16-ounce) package frozen broccoli, carrots, and
    water chestnuts
1 tablespoon cornstarch
1 tablespoon brown sugar
½ teaspoon ground ginger
½ cup soy sauce
⅓ cup pineapple juice
Hot cooked rice

Pour oil around top of a preheated wok, coating sides, or in a large nonstick skillet. Heat briefly at medium-high (375°). Add chicken and almonds; stir-fry 2 minutes. Add frozen vegetables; cover and cook 4 minutes, stirring once.

Combine cornstarch and next 4 ingredients; add to wok. Cook, stirring constantly, 2 to 3 minutes or until mixture thickens. Serve over rice. Yield: 4 servings.

Here's a **one-dish meal** for sure—chicken, veggies, and rice.

Paella

prep: 7 minutes   cook: 45 minutes

1½ pounds chicken breast strips (tenders)
2 tablespoons olive oil
2 garlic cloves, crushed
1 large onion, finely chopped
2 (14½-ounce) cans stewed tomatoes, undrained
1 (10-ounce) package saffron rice, uncooked
1 cup water
½ teaspoon dried oregano
½ teaspoon ground cumin
1 (16-ounce) package peeled frozen cooked shrimp
1 (10-ounce) package frozen sweet green peas
1 (6½-ounce) can minced clams, drained

Brown chicken in oil in a Dutch oven over medium heat. Add garlic and onion. Cook, stirring constantly, 5 minutes or until chicken is done. Stir in tomatoes and next 4 ingredients. Bring to a boil; cover, reduce heat, and simmer 25 minutes. Add frozen shrimp, peas, and clams; cover and simmer 10 more minutes. Serve immediately. Yield: 6 servings.

Paella is a Spanish one-dish meal. Saffron rice and sweet green peas keep it **colorful.**

Chicken Caesar Salad

prep: 10 minutes   cook: 6 minutes

¼ cup white wine vinegar
2 teaspoons Dijon mustard
1 teaspoon Worcestershire sauce
1½ pounds chicken breast strips (tenders)
1½ tablespoons lemon pepper
1 teaspoon garlic powder
¼ cup olive oil
8 cups tightly packed torn or shredded Romaine lettuce
    (about 1 medium head)
2 cups garlic croutons
½ cup shredded Parmesan cheese

Combine first 3 ingredients, stirring well; set aside. **Dredge** chicken in lemon pepper and garlic powder. Pour oil into a large skillet, and place over medium-high heat until hot. Cook chicken in hot oil 5 minutes or until done, turning once. Remove chicken from skillet, reserving drippings in skillet; drain chicken on paper towels. Remove skillet from heat; stir vinegar mixture into reserved drippings, scraping particles that cling to bottom of skillet. Pour warm vinegar dressing over lettuce; add chicken, and toss. Sprinkle with croutons and cheese. Yield: 4 servings.

Most stores sell **strips of chicken breast** labeled tenders, but if not, cut your own from boneless breasts.

Nacho Chicken

prep: 5 minutes   cook: 25 minutes

2   tablespoons mayonnaise
¼   teaspoon salt
¼   teaspoon dried Italian seasoning
2   skinned and boned chicken breast halves
¾   cup crushed nacho cheese-flavored tortilla chips
        (about 30)
1   tablespoon butter or margarine, melted

Combine first 3 ingredients; spread on both sides of chicken. Dredge chicken in crushed chips. Place chicken on a lightly greased baking sheet or jellyroll pan. Drizzle with butter. Bake at 350° for 20 to 25 minutes or until chicken is done. Yield: 2 servings.

Kids love this crispy chicken breaded with nacho-flavored chips.

Turkey Pie

prep: 12 minutes   cook: 45 minutes

½ (15-ounce) package refrigerated piecrusts
3 large eggs, lightly beaten
1 cup (4 ounces) shredded sharp Cheddar cheese, divided
2 cups chopped cooked turkey
⅓ cup chopped onion
⅓ cup chicken broth
¼ cup half-and-half
¼ cup mayonnaise
2 tablespoons all-purpose flour
¼ teaspoon salt
¼ teaspoon pepper
3 drops of hot sauce
1 (8-ounce) container sour cream

Fit piecrust into a 9-inch pieplate according to package directions; fold edges under, and crimp. Prick bottom and sides lightly with a fork. Bake at 400° for 10 minutes.

Combine eggs, ½ cup cheese, turkey, and remaining 9 ingredients in a large bowl, stirring until blended; pour into prepared crust. Bake, uncovered, at 400° for 20 minutes. Reduce oven temperature to 350°. Bake 10 to 15 more minutes or until set; sprinkle with remaining ½ cup cheese for last 2 minutes of baking. Yield: 6 servings.

Leftover turkey is a prize in this easy, cheesy meat pie.

Salmon Bake with Pecan-Crunch Coating

prep: 5 minutes   cook: 15 minutes

 4 salmon fillets (about 1½ inches thick)
¼ teaspoon salt
⅛ teaspoon pepper
 2 tablespoons Dijon mustard
 2 tablespoons butter or margarine, melted
1½ tablespoons honey
¼ cup soft breadcrumbs
¼ cup finely chopped pecans
 1 tablespoon chopped fresh parsley
Garnish: lemon slices

Sprinkle salmon with salt and pepper; place, skin side down, in a lightly greased 11- x 7-inch or 9-inch square baking dish.

Combine mustard, butter, and honey; brush over salmon. Combine breadcrumbs, pecans, and parsley; spoon evenly across top of salmon. Bake, uncovered, at 450° for 12 to 15 minutes or until fish flakes easily when tested with a fork. Garnish, if desired. Yield: 4 servings.

So easy. So quick. **So yummy.**

Catfish Meunière

prep: 8 minutes   cook: 8 minutes

 1 large egg, lightly beaten
 ¼ cup milk
 ½ cup all-purpose flour
 ½ teaspoon salt
 ½ teaspoon ground red pepper
 4 farm-raised catfish fillets
 ½ cup butter or margarine, divided
 ¼ cup vegetable oil
 2 tablespoons chopped fresh parsley
 2 tablespoons lemon juice
 ½ teaspoon Worcestershire sauce
    Garnishes: fresh parsley sprigs, lemon wedges

Combine egg and milk in a large shallow bowl. Combine flour, salt, and pepper in a shallow dish. Dip fish in egg mixture, and dredge in flour mixture.

Melt ¼ cup butter in a large nonstick skillet over medium heat. Add oil; increase heat to medium-high. Place fish in skillet, and cook 4 minutes on each side or until fish flakes with a fork. Drain on paper towels.

Melt remaining ¼ cup butter in skillet; stir in chopped parsley, lemon juice, and Worcestershire sauce. Spoon over fish. Garnish, if desired. Yield: 4 servings.

Meunière is a French term for fish that's lightly seasoned, dusted with flour, and pan-fried.

Shrimp Creole

prep: 8 minutes   cook: 10 minutes

2 tablespoons butter or margarine
½ cup chopped green bell pepper
¼ cup chopped celery
4 green onions, thinly sliced
1 garlic clove, minced
1 (14½-ounce) can Cajun-style stewed tomatoes,
    undrained
1 (6-ounce) can tomato paste
½ cup water
2 teaspoons dried parsley flakes
½ teaspoon chicken bouillon granules
½ teaspoon salt
¼ teaspoon ground red pepper
1 pound peeled, medium-size fresh shrimp (1⅓ pounds
    unpeeled)
Hot cooked rice

Melt butter in a large skillet over medium-high heat; add green pepper and next 3 ingredients. Cook, stirring constantly, 4 minutes. Add tomatoes and next 6 ingredients; cook 2 minutes over medium heat. Add shrimp, and cook 4 minutes or until shrimp turn pink. Serve over rice. Yield: 3 to 4 servings.

Cajun-style tomatoes provide much of the seasoning in this simple favorite.

Artichoke and Shrimp Linguine

prep: 4 minutes   cook: 18 minutes

8   ounces dried linguine, uncooked
¼   cup olive oil
1   pound peeled, medium-size fresh shrimp (1⅓ pounds
    unpeeled)
½   teaspoon dried crushed red pepper
3   garlic cloves, minced
1   (14-ounce) can quartered artichoke hearts, drained
1   (2¼-ounce) can sliced ripe olives, drained
¼   cup lemon juice
⅛   teaspoon salt
⅛   teaspoon pepper
½   cup grated Parmesan cheese

Cook pasta according to package directions; drain and
keep warm in a large bowl.

Meanwhile, heat oil in a large skillet over medium-
high heat until hot; add shrimp, red pepper, and garlic. Cook, stirring constantly, 3 to 5 minutes or until
shrimp turn pink. Stir in artichoke hearts and next 4
ingredients; cook just until thoroughly heated. Add
artichoke mixture to pasta, and sprinkle with cheese.
Yield: 4 servings.

Sauté the shrimp mixture while the pasta cooks,
and **dinner's ready in half the time.**

Scallops in Vermouth Cream

prep: 4 minutes   cook: 10 minutes

1   pound sea scallops
2   tablespoons all-purpose flour
2   tablespoons butter or margarine
¼   cup dry vermouth or other white wine
½   cup whipping cream
¼   teaspoon salt
⅛   teaspoon pepper

Toss scallops with flour. Melt butter in a large skillet over medium heat, and add scallops. Cook 4 to 5 minutes or until scallops are done and lightly browned on both sides, turning occasionally. Remove scallops from skillet.

Add vermouth to skillet, stirring to loosen browned bits from bottom of skillet; bring to a boil. Cook 2 minutes or until vermouth is reduced by half. Stir in whipping cream, salt, and pepper; reduce heat to low. Add scallops; cook just until thoroughly heated. Yield: 2 servings.

Vermouth is a white wine flavored with **herbs and spices.**

Black Beans and Yellow Rice

prep: 4 minutes   cook: 23 minutes

1   (5-ounce) package saffron rice mix
1   (15-ounce) can black beans
3   tablespoons lime juice
1   teaspoon chili powder
½   teaspoon ground cumin
2   tablespoons chopped fresh cilantro, divided
Garnishes: sour cream, sliced green onions

Cook rice according to package directions; keep warm. Meanwhile, drain beans, reserving 2 tablespoons liquid. Combine beans, reserved liquid, lime juice, chili powder, and cumin in a saucepan. Cook over medium heat until thoroughly heated; stir in 1 tablespoon cilantro.

Serve beans over rice, and sprinkle with remaining 1 tablespoon cilantro. Garnish, if desired. Yield: 3 servings.

Rice mix, a can of beans, and a few simple seasonings become **a vegetarian delight.**

Tortilla Pie

prep: 11 minutes   cook: 25 minutes

1 (16-ounce) can refried beans or black beans, drained
1 teaspoon chili powder
½ teaspoon ground cumin
8 (8-inch) flour tortillas
1 cup chunky salsa, divided
2 (4- or 6-ounce) cartons guacamole
1 (8-ounce) package shredded Mexican cheese blend
Garnishes: sour cream, additional salsa and guacamole

Combine first 3 ingredients, stirring well.

Place 1 tortilla in a lightly greased 9-inch round cakepan; spread with half of bean mixture, and top with another tortilla. Spread with ½ cup salsa, and top with another tortilla. Spread with half of guacamole, and top with another tortilla. Sprinkle with half of cheese, and top with another tortilla.

Repeat layers with remaining ingredients, except cheese. (Pan will be full.) Cover and bake at 350° for 20 minutes; uncover and sprinkle with remaining cheese.

Bake, uncovered, 3 to 5 more minutes. Cut into wedges to serve. Garnish, if desired. Yield: 6 servings.

Your salsa selection can **spice things up** or tone things down in this recipe.

index

Apples, Grilled Ham and, 32
Artichoke and Shrimp Linguine, 44

Beans and Yellow Rice, Black, 46
Beef
  Burgers, Oriental, 25
  Chili Dogs, Speedy, 17
  Enchiladas, Weeknight, 3
  Filet Mignon with Horseradish
      Gravy, 15
  Lasagna, Shortcut, 24
  Sloppy Joes, Sweet, 26
  Steak in Pepper Cream, 23
  Stew, Texas, 27
Breads
  Dilled Garlic Bread, 5
  Loaf, Sausage-Stuffed French, 13

Cheese
  Chili Dogs, Speedy, 17
  Enchiladas, Weeknight, 3
  Ham and Cheese, Grilled, 21
  Lasagna, Shortcut, 24
  Loaf, Sausage-Stuffed French, 13
Chicken
  Almond Chicken, Toasted, 34
  Casserole, Creamy Chicken, 9
  Nacho Chicken, 39
  Paella, 37
  Parmigiana, Chicken, 35
  Salad, Chicken Caesar, 38
  Stir-Fry, Chicken-Almond, 36
Coleslaw, Easy, 17
Cucumber-Tomato Salad, 13

Desserts
  Frappé, Lemon, 19
  Ice Cream, Cinnamon, 7
  Tiramisù, Simple, 11
  Toffee Surprise, 3

Enchiladas, Weeknight, 3

Fish. See also Salmon, Scallops, Shrimp.
  Catfish Meunière, 42
  Oven-Fried Fish, 19

Ham
  Apples, Grilled Ham and, 32
  Cheese, Grilled Ham and, 21
  Creamy Ham Casserole, 33

Ice Cream. See Desserts.

Ketchup, Hoisin, 25

Lasagna, Shortcut, 24
Lemon Frappé, 19
Lime Frappé, 19

Menus
  A Taste of Tex-Mex, 2
  Before the Game, 16
  Casual Night, 6
  Family-Pleasing Chicken, 8
  Faux-Fried Favorites, 18
  Italian Fare, 10
  Patio Supper, 12
  Soup and Sandwich Night, 20
  Splurge Supper, 14
  Sunset Supper, 4
Mushroom-Veal Marsala, 28

Orange and Lettuce Salad, Mandarin, 9

Pastas
  Artichoke and Shrimp Linguine, 44
  Shrimp and Pasta, Herbed, 5
Pies and Pastries
  Tortilla Pie, 47
  Turkey Pie, 40
Pork. See also Ham, Sausage.
  Cutlets, Three-Pepper Pork, 7
  Ribs, Sweet Jalapeno, 31
  Stir-Fry, Hunan Pork and Zucchini, 29
  Tenderloin, Molasses-Grilled Pork, 30

Rice, Black Beans and Yellow, 46

Salads
  Chicken Caesar Salad, 38
  Cucumber-Tomato Salad, 13
  Greek Salad, 15
  Mandarin Orange and Lettuce Salad, 9
Salmon Bake with Pecan-Crunch Coating, 41
Sandwiches
  Burgers, Oriental, 25
  Ham and Cheese, Grilled, 21
  Sloppy Joes, Sweet, 26
Sauces
  Carbonara, Quick, 11
Sausage-Stuffed French Loaf, 13
Scallops in Vermouth Cream, 45
Shrimp
  Creole, Shrimp, 43
  Linguine, Artichoke and Shrimp, 44
  Paella, 37
  Pasta, Herbed Shrimp and, 5
Soup and Stew
  Pimiento Soup, Cream of, 21
  Texas Stew, 27

Tomato Salad, Cucumber-, 13
Turkey Pie, 40

Veal Marsala, Mushroom-, 28

Zucchini Stir-Fry, Hunan Pork and, 29